Carnal Knowledge

Carnal Knowledge

A SCREENPLAY BY

Jules Feiffer

FARRAR, STRAUS AND GIROUX
NEW YORK

To Mike Nichols

CAST

JONATHAN: *Jack Nicholson*
SUSAN: *Candice Bergen*
SANDY: *Arthur Garfunkel*
BOBBIE: *Ann-Margret*
LOUISE: *Rita Moreno*
CINDY: *Cynthia O'Neal*
JENNIFER: *Carol Kane*

CREDITS

PRODUCED AND DIRECTED BY *Mike Nichols*
WRITTEN BY *Jules Feiffer*
EXECUTIVE PRODUCER *Joseph E. Levine*
ASSOCIATE PRODUCER *Clive Reed*
DIRECTOR OF PHOTOGRAPHY *Giuseppe Rotunno, A.S.C.*
FILM EDITOR *Sam O'Steen*
PRODUCTION DESIGNER *Richard Sylbert*
COSTUME DESIGNER *Anthea Sylbert*
SOUND *Lawrence O. Jost*
ASSISTANT DIRECTOR *Tim Zinnemann*
SET DECORATOR *George R. Nelson*
HAIR STYLES *Sydney Guilaroff*
ART DIRECTOR *Robert Luthardt*

Filmed in Panavision   Color by Technicolor
An Avco Embassy release

Carnal Knowledge

Credits

Throughout the credits we hear the off-screen voices of JONATHAN and SANDY, low and very close.

Sound: In the background—dance music of the forties.

JONATHAN

If you had the choice—

SANDY

Yeah?

JONATHAN

Would you rather love a girl or have her love you?

SANDY

I'd want it mutual—

JONATHAN

I mean if you couldn't have it mutual.

SANDY

You mean, would I rather be the one who loves or is loved?

JONATHAN

Yeah.

SANDY

It's not that easy a question. I think I'd rather be in love.

JONATHAN

Me, too. I wouldn't want to get hurt, though. Every time I start being in love, the girl does something that turns me cold.

SANDY

You were in love with Gloria.

JONATHAN

I started to be in love. And then she let me feel her up on the first date. It turned me right off.

SANDY

You kept going with her.

JONATHAN

Well, she let me feel her up.

SANDY

Yeah? What about Gwen?

JONATHAN

Her, I could talk to.

SANDY

I've never been able to talk to any girl.

JONATHAN

I was really getting crazy about her, but she was stuck-up. She wouldn't let me lay a hand on her. So I went back to Gloria.

SANDY

You want perfection.

JONATHAN

What do you want, wise guy?

SANDY

She just has to be nice. That's all.

JONATHAN

You don't want her beautiful?

SANDY

She doesn't have to be beautiful. I'd like her built,
though.

JONATHAN

I'd want mine sexy-looking.

SANDY

I wouldn't want her to look like a tramp.

JONATHAN

Sexy doesn't mean she has to look like a tramp.
There's a middle ground.

SANDY

I'd want that, yeah.

JONATHAN

Tall, very tall.

SANDY

(*A nervous laugh*) That would scare me.

JONATHAN

She should be very understanding. We'd start the
same sentences together.

SANDY

I'd like to do that.

JONATHAN

Big tits.

SANDY

Yeah. But still a virgin.

JONATHAN

I don't care about that.

SANDY

Come on!

JONATHAN

I wouldn't mind if she was just a little ahead of me
—with those big tits—and knew hundreds of different ways—

SANDY

I want more of a companion. That other stuff I can
get on the outside.

JONATHAN

The first time I do it I want it beautiful. I don't
want to waste it on some beast.

SANDY

I feel the same way about getting laid as I feel about
going to college. I'm being pressured into it.

Fade in on interior: college dance—night
Smith College in October of 1946

SUSAN enters, walks past JONATHAN and SANDY, who *stare*
after her.

Sound: The music continues as before.

JONATHAN

You like that?

SANDY

Yeah!

JONATHAN

I give her to you.

SANDY

What's wrong with her?

JONATHAN

I'm a generous guy.

SANDY

I'm grateful. How do I break the news to her?

JONATHAN

You go over there—

SANDY

Yeah—

JONATHAN

There is a way to talk to girls. Tell her a joke.

SANDY

What joke?

JONATHAN

Tell her about your unhappy childhood.

SANDY

Hey, that's not bad.

JONATHAN

But don't make it like an act.

SANDY

No—

Go ahead! Go ahead, schmuck!

Pause.

JONATHAN

If you don't, I will.

SANDY

You? You can't even stand up.

A pause. SANDY walks over to SUSAN and stares dumbly at her.

Sound: The music breaks. A moment of soft, unexcited party noise.

SUSAN stares back at SANDY, inquiringly.

Sound: The music begins.

SANDY turns away from SUSAN. *Follow him* as he walks over to JONATHAN.

Angle on Sandy and Jonathan

SANDY

I fucked up.

JONATHAN

It's my turn.

SANDY

Whadayamean it's your turn? She's mine! You gave her to me!

JONATHAN

You struck out.

SANDY

I get two more times at bat.

JONATHAN watches as SANDY turns his back on him and approaches SUSAN.

SANDY reaches SUSAN and stands there paralyzed.

Angle on Sandy and Susan

SUSAN

This is the first time I've ever been to a college mixer.

SANDY

(*Awakening hope*) Me, too. I hate them.

SUSAN

I hate them too.

SANDY

It's such a phony way of meeting people.

SUSAN

Everybody puts on an act.

SANDY

So, even if you meet somebody, you don't know who you're meeting.

SUSAN

Because you're meeting the act.

SANDY

That's right. Not the person.

SUSAN

I'm not sure I agree.

SANDY

With what?

SUSAN

With what you said.

SANDY

No, I don't either.

SUSAN

You don't agree with what you said?

SANDY

(Cautious) How do you feel about it?

SUSAN

I think people only like to think they're putting on an act, but it's not an act, it's really them. If they think it's an act they feel better because they think they can always change it.

SANDY

You mean they're kidding themselves because it's not really an act.

SUSAN

Yes, it is an act. But they're the act. The act is them.

SANDY

But if it's them, then how can it be an act?

SUSAN

Because *they're* an act.

SANDY

But they're also real.

SUSAN

No.

SANDY

You mean I'm not real?

SUSAN

No.

SANDY

(Hurt) I'm an act.

SUSAN

It's all right. I'm an act too. Don't you behave differently with different people?

SANDY

No.

SUSAN

With your family?

SANDY

Oh, I thought you meant different people. Well, sure, my family—

SUSAN

And with your friends, you're another way.

SANDY

Well, sure, my friends—

SUSAN

And with your teachers, you're still another way. So which one is you?

SANDY

(Laughs) Well, when you put it that way. *(Laughs)* You ought to be a lawyer.

SUSAN

I'm going to be a lawyer.

SANDY

A lady lawyer.

SUSAN doesn't answer. A pause.

SANDY

Um—you're from Smith, right?

She nods.

SANDY

Do you like it?

SUSAN

I like it all right. Do you like Amherst?

SANDY

Sure, why shouldn't I? My parents worked very hard to send me. *(Laughs)* I'd better like it. *(Pause)* Do you have a name or something?

SUSAN

Susan.

SANDY

I'm Sandy.

Cut to:

Interior: Jonathan and Sandy's dormitory room—night

SANDY and JONATHAN are in bed.

JONATHAN

I think you can make out with her.

SANDY

You think so?

JONATHAN

She's stuff.

SANDY

You think so?

JONATHAN

I wouldn't kick her out of bed.

SANDY

I shouldn't try somebody else?

JONATHAN

Who?

SANDY

She was the best-looking girl at the whole mixer, I'll say that for her. *(Uncertainly)* Wasn't she?

JONATHAN

Her tits were too small.

SANDY

I was thinking of that. The hell with her.

JONATHAN

But her legs were great.

SANDY

You think so? Standing so close, I couldn't really tell about her legs.

JONATHAN

I wouldn't kick her out of bed.

SANDY

She's got some funny ideas.

JONATHAN

I wouldn't kick her out of bed.

Cut to:

Exterior: Smith campus—night

SUSAN and SANDY are standing together, almost hidden in the tree shadows. SUSAN is breaking out of SANDY's embrace.

SUSAN

Don't rush me.

SANDY

What's the matter? I like you very much, Susan.

He tries unsuccessfully to kiss her.

SANDY

It's our third date.

SUSAN takes his hand.

SUSAN

I like you too.

SANDY

You let me kiss you last week.

SUSAN

And this week.

SANDY

If I could kiss you once last week, I should be able to kiss you at least twice tonight.

SUSAN

(Smiles) You're the only boy I know who I can talk to.

14

SANDY

I can't see you being quiet for any guy.

SUSAN

Not quiet, exactly. But if you know somebody's not going to approve of what you are—

SANDY

Whatever that is.

SUSAN

Whatever that is. If you know that, well, you just don't tell him. If I like a boy, if I want him to keep liking me and I'm brighter than he is, I have to not show it or I'll lose him. So it's hard.

SANDY

Well, I wouldn't want anyone overly bright.

SUSAN

But you wouldn't feel threatened—

SANDY

I might be bothered a little.

SUSAN

I don't think you would, nearly as much as some people. For example, some day I want to write novels. Not now, but when I have something to say. Now that doesn't threaten you, does it?

SANDY

No. *(A pause)* A little.

He looks at her with great admiration. She smiles warmly. He quickly leans forward to kiss her.

SUSAN

Don't press so hard.

They kiss.

SUSAN

See, it's better when it's gentle.

They kiss.

SUSAN

See? What are you grinning at?

Cut to:

Interior: Jonathan and Sandy's dorm bathroom—morning
Close-up: Jonathan in the shower

JONATHAN

You feel her up yet?

Full shot of bathroom

SANDY is shaving.

SANDY

Come on, I like this girl.

JONATHAN

Was I right about kissing her?

SANDY

Listen, we had a big fight over it.

JONATHAN

And you won.

SANDY

Well, I don't know if I won or not—

JONATHAN

Why do you let yourself be pushed around?

SANDY

You're the one who's pushing me around! Well, I guess I won. Sure, I won. She kissed me five times.

JONATHAN

That's when you should've put your hand on her tit.

SANDY

Come on—when this girl's nice enough to kiss me, I should do that to her?

JONATHAN

You act as if she's doing you a favor.

SANDY

Well, it is sort of a favor. Isn't it? I mean when a girl lets you kiss her and, you know, go on from there—feel her up and, you know, the rest of it, go all the way and the rest of it, I mean isn't it a favor? What's in it for her? I mean if she's not getting paid or anything?

JONATHAN starts to laugh.

SANDY

Fuck you!

JONATHAN roars with laughter.

SANDY

Okay, okay, I'll feel her up!

Exterior: woods—late afternoon

Bright sunlight through the trees. SUSAN and SANDY.

> SUSAN
>
> Sandy, please take your hand off my breast.

> SANDY
>
> Why?

> SUSAN
>
> Because I want you to.

He doesn't move.

> SUSAN
>
> How can it be any fun for you when you know I don't want it?

> SANDY
>
> I didn't say it was fun.

> SUSAN
>
> Then why is your hand where it is?

> SANDY
>
> Because the way we're going, by this time I should be feeling you up.

> SUSAN
>
> I don't feel that way about you, Sandy.

> SANDY
>
> I feel that way about you.

SUSAN

But you want me to feel something for you too, don't you?

SANDY

I thought you liked me.

SUSAN

I do like you, but I like you for other reasons.

SANDY

So?

SUSAN

If we went any further, there wouldn't be those reasons any more.

SANDY

Well, we might have something else, though.

SUSAN

What?

SANDY shrugs.

SANDY

Something else. You're the first girl I've ever done that to, Susan.

SUSAN

I didn't know that.

SANDY

It doesn't show?

SUSAN

No.

SANDY

Well, it's something we both have to go through.

SUSAN smiles. She puts his hand on her breast. He takes it away.

> SANDY
>
> Susan, are you a virgin?

She nods. He puts his hand back on her breast.

> SANDY
>
> What do I do with my other hand?

She puts it on her other breast.

> SANDY
>
> What are you gonna do with *your* hands?

> *Cut to:*

Exterior: Amherst campus—night

JONATHAN and SANDY are walking down the street that leads to their dorm. Fall leaves cover the ground.

> JONATHAN
>
> And then what?

> SANDY
>
> She told me to take my hand off her breast.

> JONATHAN
>
> And then what?

> SANDY
>
> I said I didn't want to.

> JONATHAN
>
> And then what?

SANDY

She said how could it be fun for me when she didn't
like it.

JONATHAN

(Disgusted) Jesus!

SANDY

So I said, I thought you liked me.

JONATHAN

Yeah?

SANDY

And she said, I like you for other reasons.

JONATHAN

Other reasons?!

SANDY

So I told her how I really needed this.

JONATHAN

What did you tell her?

SANDY

You know—that it was my first time.

JONATHAN

Your first time what? What did you say exactly?

SANDY

I don't remember exactly—that she's the first girl I
ever tried to feel up.

JONATHAN

You told her that?

SANDY

Was it a mistake?

21

JONATHAN shrugs.

> JONATHAN
>
> I wouldn't.

> SANDY
>
> Then she got nicer to me.

> JONATHAN
>
> What do you mean, nicer?

> SANDY
>
> She put my hand on her breast.

> JONATHAN
>
> You mean you put it on and she left it.

> SANDY
>
> No, she picked it up and put it on.

> JONATHAN
>
> She picked up your hand like this—

Mimes motion with his own hand.

> JONATHAN
>
> —and put it on like this?

Puts hand on his own breast.

> SANDY
>
> That's right. So I didn't know what to think.

JONATHAN leers.

> JONATHAN
>
> You didn't, huh?

> SANDY
>
> I mean from just wanting to be friends, she's sud-
> denly getting pretty aggressive.

JONATHAN

And then what?

SANDY

I asked her if she was a virgin.

JONATHAN

(Laughs) You're kidding!

SANDY

Was that a mistake?

JONATHAN shrugs.

SANDY

Anyhow, she is.

JONATHAN

She says. So now you got what? One hand, or two hands, on her tits?

SANDY

By this time she's put the other hand on her other one.

JONATHAN

She put *both* hands on?

SANDY nods.

JONATHAN

Two hands?

SANDY nods.

SANDY

So I said, what are you gonna do with *your* hands?

JONATHAN

(Laughs) You didn't say that.

SANDY

(Pleased) It just came out!

JONATHAN

Then what?

SANDY

She . . . let me see if I got this right—yeah—she un-
zipped my fly.

JONATHAN

Bullshit artist!

He slaps his hands together.

JONATHAN

And then what?

A spreading grin from SANDY.

JONATHAN

Then what?!

SANDY

She did it.

JONATHAN

Did *what?*

SANDY makes a hand motion indicating masturbation.

JONATHAN

Bullshit artist!

SANDY shakes his head, grinning.

JONATHAN

She really did *that?*

SANDY is virtually jumping up and down in excitement. He

and JONATHAN begin to giggle. The giggle explodes into a
roar.

> JONATHAN
> She did *that?!*

Cut to:

Interior: telephone booth—night
Close-up: Jonathan

> JONATHAN
> Hello, is this Susan? Well, you don't know me, I'm a
> friend of Sandy's, his roommate. Yeah, Jonathan.
> He told you about me? Yeah—so I'm just here at
> Smith for tonight—practically on campus. I was tak-
> ing a drive, you know—and I found myself practi-
> cally on campus . . .

Cut to:

Exterior: Susan's sorority house—night

Move back with SUSAN and JONATHAN as they cross the
street away from the sorority house.

For a long moment, neither has anything to say.

> JONATHAN
> Do you like Smith?

> SUSAN
> What's your major?

Interior: Jonathan's car—night

JONATHAN is driving.

> JONATHAN
>
> Where'd you go to high school?

> SUSAN
>
> Where do you go in the summer?

> JONATHAN
>
> Do you always answer a question with a question?

> SUSAN
>
> Do you always date your best friends' girl friends?

> JONATHAN
>
> Sandy told me you were beautiful.

> SUSAN
>
> He told me you were sexy. I guess he's just a poor judge.

> JONATHAN
>
> I guess what he meant is you've got personality.

> SUSAN
>
> Good grief!

> JONATHAN
>
> You have a special quality. I like girls who are special.

> SUSAN
>
> I'm hardly that special.

Cut to:

Interior: college-town bar—night

The bar is jammed with students. JONATHAN and SUSAN are seated at a table, drinking beer.

> JONATHAN
>
> Some people you can tell about right away. Most girls I talk to, it's like we're both spies from foreign countries and we're speaking in code. Everything means something else. Like I say, "Would you like to take a walk?" and it means something else. And she says, "I can't, I've got a French test tomorrow," and it means something else.

> SUSAN
>
> And you say, "I'll come over and help you study," and it means something else.

> JONATHAN
>
> You're very sharp. I like that.

> SUSAN
>
> And that means something else.

> JONATHAN
>
> You're too sharp.

> SUSAN
>
> Does that bother you?

> JONATHAN
>
> It interests me.

> SUSAN
>
> Is that more code?

> JONATHAN
>
> We'd be good together.

SUSAN

I'm dating your best friend.

JONATHAN

He won't mind.

SUSAN

How do you know?

JONATHAN

I won't tell him.

SUSAN

What if I mind?

JONATHAN

Do you wanna go out Friday?

SUSAN

I'm seeing Sandy.

JONATHAN

Saturday?

SUSAN

I have a date.

JONATHAN

Sunday?

SUSAN

I'm seeing my folks.

JONATHAN

Where do they live?

SUSAN

Newton.

JONATHAN

Sunday night.

I'll be too tired.

JONATHAN

I'll help you get over your folks.

SUSAN smiles.

JONATHAN

How about it, Susan? What are you so afraid of?

SUSAN laughs.

SUSAN

Not you.

Cut to:

Interior: Jonathan and Sandy's dormitory room— morning

JONATHAN is asleep. SANDY lies awake in bed, staring at the ceiling.

SANDY

I think I'm in love. *(No response. He tries again)* I think I'm in love.

JONATHAN

(Slowly wakening) Bullshit artist.

SANDY

I really think so.

JONATHAN

You get in yet?

SANDY

What's that got to do with it?

JONATHAN

How do you know if you don't know how you are in bed together?

SANDY

That's not everything.

JONATHAN

It's a lot.

SANDY

She tells me thoughts that I didn't even know I had, until she tells them to me. It's unbelievable! I can talk to her!

JONATHAN

You can talk to me too. Are you in love with me?

SANDY

I can say things to her I wouldn't dare say to you.

JONATHAN

What, for instance?

SANDY

Things you'd laugh at.

JONATHAN

Listen, I'm laughing now.

SANDY

She thinks I'm sensitive.

JONATHAN

Sensitive. *(Laughs)* Oh boy! Sensitive! *(Laughs)* What do you talk to her about? Flowers?

SANDY

Books.

JONATHAN

Books? You phony. I read more books than you do.

SANDY

I'm going to start. I'm reading *The Fountainhead.*

JONATHAN

The Fountainhead? What's that?

SANDY

It's her favorite book. You ever hear of *Jean Christophe?*

JONATHAN

What's that?

SANDY

It's a classic, you moron. I'm going to read it right after *The Fountainhead.*

JONATHAN

Yeah—you ever read *Guadalcanal Diary* by Richard Tregaskis?

SANDY

No.

JONATHAN

That was a best-seller, and I read it. You ever read *Gentleman's Agreement* by Laura Z. Hobson? You ever read *A Bell for Adano* by John Hersey?

SANDY

I'm going to read everything from now on.

JONATHAN

I read a lot more than you. So who's the one who's sensitive? You or me? Come on! Who's sensitive?!

SANDY stares at him, puzzled by the sudden outburst.

Cut to:

Interior: Jonathan's parked car—night

JONATHAN
(To SUSAN*)* I've had a very messed-up childhood.

SUSAN
What does your father do?

JONATHAN
He fails.

She laughs.

JONATHAN
It's not funny.

SUSAN
(Sobers immediately) Were you very poor?

JONATHAN
My father couldn't hold on to a job. He kept giving
me advice. The more he failed, the more advice I
got. He's a Communist, my father.

SUSAN
We're Republicans. Sometimes I think I'm a Communist.

JONATHAN
Me, too. We have so much and other people have,
you know, so little. After I get set up as a lawyer,
what I'd really like to do is get into politics. Public

service. What really gets me is I was too young to fight in the war because what was that all about except to show that if everybody pitches in, the plain people have a chance; so even though I'm the first in my family to get an education, I don't ever want to forget where I came from.

SUSAN turns and stares at him.

SUSAN

You're a lot more serious than I thought.

JONATHAN

I know.

Cut to:

Exterior: library—night

Move back with JONATHAN and SANDY as they skip down library steps.

SANDY

Where'd you meet her?

JONATHAN

I'm another person with her. You wouldn't recognize me. The things that come out of my mouth—

SANDY

Hey, she really sounds like something. Is she built?

JONATHAN

She—she's got a quality—she doesn't talk much, but the things she has to say are so sharp.

33

Interior: Jonathan and Sandy's dormitory room—night

The boys are in bed. The lights are out. JONATHAN smokes quietly. After a pause:

> SANDY
>
> We should double-date sometime.

> JONATHAN
>
> Well, I want to know her a little better, y'know, before we double-date.

> SANDY
>
> Gee, isn't it great? A month ago neither of us even knew a girl. What's her name?

Pause.

> JONATHAN
>
> Myrtle.

Cut to:

Exterior: woods—night
Close-up

On JONATHAN and SUSAN in mid-fuck. SUSAN gasps, JONATHAN groans. Then they are still. JONATHAN rolls off her. SUSAN sits up quickly, then lies down again in JONATHAN's arms. JONATHAN looks over at her, then grins up at the sky.

Cut to:

Interior: gymnasium swimming pool—morning
Close-up: Sandy in the pool

>   SANDY
> Bullshit artist!

Pull back to full shot of the pool. SANDY is grinning up at
JONATHAN, who stands at the edge of the pool, still in the
same clothes he wore during his night with SUSAN. JONA-
THAN lets out a cowboy yell and leaps into the pool. He
hugs and ducks SANDY.

>   SANDY
> You're kidding me—you're not kidding me—you
> really did it? You beat me to it, you bastard! You
> bastard! Finding a girl who puts out!

Interior: gym locker room

JONATHAN, still clothed and soaking wet, walks SANDY to
his locker. SANDY starts to dress.

>   SANDY
> Next it's my turn!

>   JONATHAN
> I don't think she'll do it, Sandy.

>   SANDY
> She will! I've just been taking it easy with her.

>   JONATHAN
> Sandy, believe me, find somebody else.

>   SANDY
> Are you crazy, when I'm right on the verge? I see
> her tomorrow night!

JONATHAN

Uh—Sandy, do you ever talk to her about me?

SANDY

Yeah. Sure. Sometimes.

JONATHAN

Uh—Sandy, will you do me a favor?

SANDY

What?

JONATHAN

Don't tell her I got laid.

Cut to:

Interior: Jonathan and Sandy's dormitory room—day

SUSAN, half dressed, lies on SANDY's bed. SANDY, in his shirt, his pants off, lies next to her.

SANDY

Please, Susan.

SUSAN

Sometimes I want to do it and a second later I don't want to do it.

SANDY

Let's do it.

SUSAN

I don't know why you put up with me. I don't think I can do it.

SANDY

It really hurts, Susan.

SUSAN

Let me—

She puts her hand on his thigh.

SANDY

Not any more.

He removes her hand.

SUSAN

Please, Sandy.

SANDY

Not any more. Oh, Susan, let's do it.

A pause.

SANDY

I love you!

SUSAN stares at him.

SUSAN

Do you have anything?

SANDY, never taking his eyes off her, slips a condom out of the bed-table drawer. SUSAN cannot look.

SUSAN

How long have you had that?

SANDY

Not too long.

SUSAN

Not a year or anything—

SANDY

I'm sure it's okay.

I don't want to take any chances.

SANDY

These things have to be okay.

She doesn't answer.

SANDY

It's okay.

She doesn't respond.

SANDY

I'm positive it's okay.

Cut to:

Exterior: Amherst street—day

JONATHAN and SANDY are walking out of class. Snow is on the ground.

JONATHAN

It's as if you're the first guy in history who ever got laid.

SANDY

I'm the first guy in *my* history who ever got laid.

JONATHAN

I like it too, but you don't hear me crowing about it. There's such a thing as good taste, you know.

SANDY

What's the matter with you?

JONATHAN

Jesus!

SANDY

After *you* started scoring, what did I get out of you? We did it standing, sitting, in the car, under the car —Myrtle, Myrtle, Myrtle—maybe you forget, but I knew Susan before you knew Myrtle, and who scored first? You!! That didn't make me feel very good, you know. In fact, it made me feel very jealous. But did I try to shut you up? Did *I* say "I'm tired of hearing about it already"? I didn't say it. Because I'm your friend. So I sat through it.

JONATHAN

Okay. Okay.

SANDY

Jesus!

JONATHAN

You made your point.

SANDY

Sometimes I think I'm a better friend to you than you are to me.

Cut to:

Interior: college bar—night

Sound: Juke-box music.

SANDY and SUSAN are doing the lindy. Other couples pass in front and behind them. SANDY dances with a certain precision, as if he's counting off the beats in his head. He and SUSAN smile at each other with affection.

A couple passes in front of them, blocking our vision. The couple moves off and now it is JONATHAN doing the lindy with SUSAN. The carefree JONATHAN swings her in and out. SUSAN looks at him adoringly.

Again our view is blocked by another couple. When they move off, SUSAN is back with SANDY. They are having a good clean time.

Cut to:

Close-up on SUSAN sitting at a table, drinking a beer. JONATHAN and SANDY are seated on either side of her but are not seen. SUSAN is in the middle of a laugh.

> SANDY
>
> Didn't you ever do that? Of course, I knew what the word "misled" meant, but I didn't know what it looked like. So when I finally saw it in print I thought it was "myzeld." "He had been myzeld." "She myzeld the youth." I kept wondering: What could it mean? This word "myzeld."

> JONATHAN
>
> Sexy! "Let's myzel."

SUSAN and SANDY laugh.

> JONATHAN
>
> Does anybody know who Round John Virgin is?

> SANDY
>
> One of the guys in Robin Hood.

> SUSAN
>
> (*Correcting him*) That's Little John.

> SANDY
>
> What'd you say? Round John?

Round John Virgin.

SANDY

Is that in Falstaff?

SUSAN

(Suddenly) Round John Virgin mother and child!

She laughs, delighted with herself.

JONATHAN

Yeah!

SANDY

(Not comprehending) Round John Virgin mother—

SUSAN

(Singing) Holy infant so tender and mild—

SANDY

(Finally getting it) Oh!

All laugh.

SANDY

Gunshee!

SUSAN

Gunshee?

SANDY

G - U - N - S - H - Y. Gunshee!

JONATHAN

(Laughs) Gun shy!

SANDY

I always read it "gunshee"! Say, Susan, do the one about the bear! You'll love this, Jonathan.

SUSAN

The hymn we used to sing in church about a bear with crossed eyes—

JONATHAN

What are you giving me?

SUSAN

—whose name was Gladly.

JONATHAN

Gladly the bear?

SUSAN

You don't know it? "Gladly the Cross-Eyed Bear."

SANDY

"Gladly the Cross-Eyed Bear"—get it? Get it?

JONATHAN

(Suddenly getting it) "Gladly the Cross I'd Bear"!

All roar.

SANDY

All right. Pronounce this:
C - H - O
P - H - O
U - S - E

SUSAN

Chofoos?

JONATHAN

Chofus?

SANDY

(Beaming) Chop house!

Cut to:

Exterior: Smith campus—night

JONATHAN

(*To* SUSAN) This has to stop.

SUSAN

I don't know how to tell him.

JONATHAN

You don't have any trouble telling him lots of other things.

SUSAN

What does that mean?

JONATHAN

The way you talk to him. I don't hear you ever talking to me that way.

SUSAN

What way?

JONATHAN

I don't know.

SUSAN

He's very vulnerable. I don't want to hurt him.

JONATHAN

You're hurting me.

SUSAN

He loves me.

JONATHAN

That's no reason to go to bed with him.

She turns away.

JONATHAN

And you woulda just gone on, wouldn't you? If he hadn't of told me?

SUSAN

I don't know.

JONATHAN

I wouldn't of known a thing about it.

SUSAN

I don't know. Maybe.

JONATHAN

Boy, you're really something.

SUSAN

I don't feel like something. I feel like nothing.

JONATHAN

How much longer do you expect me to take this?

SUSAN

I'm trying to tell him.

JONATHAN

I see how you're trying!

SUSAN

It's not my fault. I don't enjoy these fights.

JONATHAN

Listen, it's me you're supposed to be in love with. I'm gonna tell him.

SUSAN

What?!

JONATHAN

I'm gonna tell him about you and me!

SUSAN

No, Jonathan!

JONATHAN

Why don't you give me some of the understanding
you give him?

SUSAN

You're stronger.

JONATHAN

You tell him everything else—you can tell him
about us!

SUSAN

What do you mean I tell him everything? Who says
so?

JONATHAN

He tells me! He's my best friend! Are you gonna
tell him?

SUSAN

He's so helpless.

She turns away.

JONATHAN

Susan, I love you! Why can't you be more with me
like you are with Sandy?

She looks at him.

Cut to:

Interior: Jonathan and Sandy's dormitory room—night

JONATHAN and SANDY in bed.

> SANDY
>
> She says she's no good for me.

> JONATHAN
>
> Maybe she's trying to let you down easy.

SANDY laughs.

> JONATHAN
>
> Go ahead and laugh. It adds up.

SANDY laughs.

> JONATHAN
>
> Go ahead and laugh.

> *Cut to:*

Interior: Susan's sorority-house common room—morning

SUSAN, her arms loaded with books, stands with JONATHAN. He needs a shave.

> JONATHAN
>
> You don't know every mood of mine like you know every mood of his.

> SUSAN
>
> No.

> JONATHAN
>
> How come?

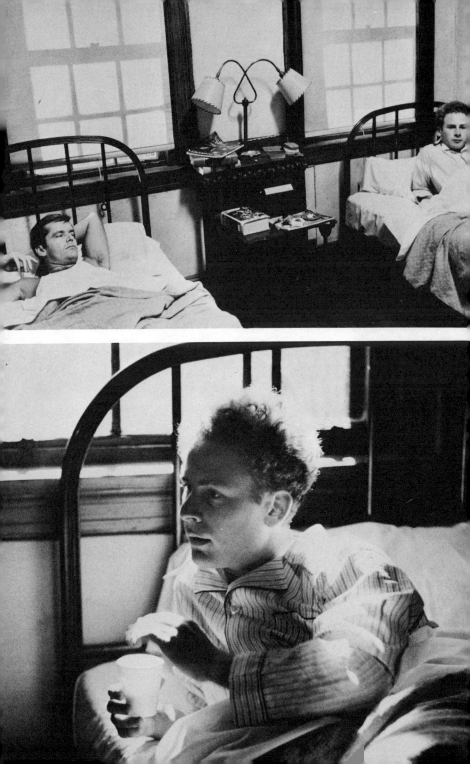

SUSAN

I don't know.

JONATHAN

You don't tell me thoughts I never knew I had.

SUSAN

Does he say I do that?

He nods.

SUSAN

Then I guess I must.

JONATHAN

You do it all right. So do it with me.

SUSAN

I can't.

JONATHAN

You can do it with him, you can do it with me. Tell me my thoughts!

SUSAN

I can't.

JONATHAN

Why can't you?

SUSAN

I can't with you.

JONATHAN

This has gone far enough.

SUSAN

I can't stand any more ultimatums, Jonathan.

JONATHAN

This is my last one! Tonight you tell him about us
or tomorrow I tell him! Look at me, Susan.

She looks at him.

JONATHAN

Now, tell me my goddamned thoughts!

Cut to:

Interior: Susan's sorority house—night

SUSAN, in a bathrobe, walks down the hall to the telephone,
which hangs off the hook. She picks it up.

SUSAN

Hello.

Intercut close-ups of JONATHAN and SUSAN.

JONATHAN

You didn't do it, did you?

SUSAN

No.

JONATHAN

Why not?

SUSAN

He looks at me with such trust.

JONATHAN

How do I look at you?

SUSAN

With bitterness.

JONATHAN

It used to be trust. At least you know my thoughts.

SUSAN

Did you tell him?

JONATHAN

What do you think?

SUSAN

No.

JONATHAN

So what do we do now?

SUSAN

I don't know. I guess I get an ultimatum.

JONATHAN

Do you think there's any sense in this?

SUSAN

In what?

JONATHAN

In you and me?

SUSAN

That's up to you.

JONATHAN

No. It's up to you—*(Pause)* I don't think there's any point—I wish I were wrong— *(Pause)* I don't feel anything any more.

SUSAN

Neither do I.

JONATHAN

The reason I didn't say anything to Sandy—I knew he wouldn't believe me. And I'd go into details so he'd have to believe me. And I knew he'd come running to you. And I knew you'd tell him everything I said was true. And I knew then you'd go to bed with him.

SUSAN

Yes. That sounds like what would happen.

A long pause.

JONATHAN

So.

SUSAN

So. Jonathan.

He listens.

SUSAN

I'll always be your friend.

JONATHAN

Jesus, Susan—I hope not.

Cut to:

Interior: Jonathan and Sandy's dormitory room—day
Close-up: Jonathan

Sounds of packing as SUSAN and SANDY are heard bustling about.

SANDY

It's going to be buggy.

SUSAN

It won't be buggy.

SANDY

It's the tropics!—what do you mean! It's the jungle!

SUSAN

You can't cover yourself from head to toe!

SANDY

I'll get eaten alive!

SUSAN

You don't know what it's like. You never camped
out before. Isn't he being silly, Jonathan?

SANDY

I am not.

SUSAN

You are too.

SANDY

Am not.

SUSAN

Are too. You're a real city boy.

SANDY

How about the cot?

SUSAN

Come on, sweetie! We've got a sleeping bag.

SANDY

You're really serious about sleeping on the ground?

SUSAN

You are a baby.

SANDY

Christ! This knapsack's heavy.

I told you—you overpacked. What in the world do you plan to do with a pillow case?

SANDY

Put it back!

SUSAN

(Laughing) You are a nut! Isn't he a nut, Jonathan?

The sound fades as they continue to bicker. JONATHAN looks directly into the camera. A long pause. JONATHAN fades as the screen bleaches to white.

Sound: Skater music.

Fade in on ice skater—day

Young, beautiful, incredibly built. She is costumed in the fashion of the early sixties. She glides heart-fetchingly toward us, away from us, back and forth across the ice, executing a series of graceful figures. This goes on for a while. *Pull back* to show JONATHAN and SANDY looking down on the Wollman Skating Rink in Central Park. They are fifteen years older. JONATHAN looks it. SANDY does not. Both are well dressed in the style of the early sixties.

JONATHAN

Jesus!—You want her?

SANDY

I wouldn't kick her out of bed.

JONATHAN

Will you look at the pair on her?

SANDY

Get a look at that schmuck trying to keep up with
her.

JONATHAN

They're always with guys like that.

SANDY

That guy must be sixty if he's a day.

JONATHAN

Maybe he'll have a heart attack, you can save his
life, get her number and fuck her.

SANDY

(Grinning) You bastard!

JONATHAN

(Grinning) You bastard! How's Susan?

SANDY

Couldn't be better.

JONATHAN

I always said it and I say it now: you found yourself
a jewel.

A pause.

SANDY

She is a jewel.

A pall. SANDY's eyes move back to the ice skater.

JONATHAN

Not bad, that one, is she?

SANDY

Listen, you must be getting more than your share.

JONATHAN

She wouldn't remember me. She's a real ball-buster, that one. I been through the mill with her kind.

SANDY

Yeah?

His eyes begin to wander.

JONATHAN

You think a girl really goes for you and you find out she's out for your money or your balls or your money and your balls. The women today are better hung than the men.

SANDY

I should have your problems.

JONATHAN

Listen, it's not as easy getting laid as it used to be. I don't think I fuck more than a dozen new girls a year now. Maybe I'm too much of a perfectionist. This last one came so close to being what I wanted. A good pair of tits on her but not a great pair; almost no ass at all and that bothered me; sensational legs—I would've settled for the legs if she had two more inches here . . . *(Indicates height)* and three more inches here. *(Indicates bust)* So anyhow that took two years out of my life.

SANDY

You don't want a family?

JONATHAN

I don't want to put it down, but who needs it?

SANDY

You can't make fucking your life's work.

JONATHAN

(Annoyed) Don't tell me what I can or can't do. You're so well-off?

Cut to:

Interior: Jonathan's office—day
Close-up: Sandy

SANDY

Susan's a very good homemaker. Very efficient. I go home, everything's in its place. Which I like. Because it's tiring putting in a full day at the office, then Doctors Hospital for a couple of hours. So it's nice to have everything in its place when I get home; a martini, dinner, the kids—we don't watch much television—we like to read aloud to each other. We used to have more friends than we do but we don't have that many any more, so on weekends we might entertain a little or go over to a friend's, or come into town to see a play or a good film. It's not glamorous or anything.

Shot: Jonathan sitting at his desk, listening